LMS Album

No. 2

A typical Midland scene from pre Stanier days. Rebuilt Johnson MR class 3P 4-4-0 No 767 pilots LMS built three-cylinder compound 4-4-0 No 1185 on a six coach Leeds-St Pancras express seen leaving Nottingham in 1932.
[*T. G. Hepburn*

Not quite so typical of the North Western is the super power employed on the 4 pm Euston-Liverpool express hauled by Bowen-Cooke LNWR "Claughton" class 5P 4-6-0 No 5938 and LMS "Royal Scot" 4-6-0 No 6147 *Courier* photographed near Bourne End box, Berkhamsted in June 1928.
[*F. R. Hebron*

BRIAN STEPHENSON

LMS Album

No. 2

LONDON

IAN ALLAN LTD

First published 1971
Second Impression 1974

ISBN 0 7110 0264 9

© Brian Stephenson, 1971

Published by Ian Allan Ltd, Shepperton, Surrey
and printed in the United Kingdom by
Ian Allan (Printing) Ltd.

Introduction

This LMS Album No 2 was originally envisaged as a successor to the LMS Album compiled by C. C. Dorman and first published in 1967 and now out of print. It was to illustrate all the various locomotive types built by the LMS, as well as present a good selection of the pre-grouping classes, but as work progressed it became increasingly clear that it would be impossible to do justice to both these aims. As I had already received a vast number of excellent pictures of pre-grouping locomotives I approached the Publisher with the suggestion that this album be devoted entirely to the locomotives inherited by the LMS in 1923—a suggestion that was enthusiastically accepted. The standard LMS engines will be fully dealt with in a third LMS Album at a future date together with, it is hoped, a selection of photographs of rolling stock, stations and signals etc.

The fact that the London Midland & Scottish Railway was the largest of the four companies set up as a result of the grouping of Britain's railways under the Railways Act, 1921, hardly bears repeating. The principal constituents of the LMS were as follows, in order of wholly owned route mileage. The London & North Western Railway which included the North London Railway which had been worked by the LNWR from 1909, the Midland Railway which included the former London Tilbury & Southend Railway taken over in 1912, the Caledonian Railway, Lancashire & Yorkshire Railway, Highland Railway, Glasgow & South Western Railway, North Staffordshire Railway and the Furness Railway. The Lancashire & Yorkshire Railway had amalgamated with the LNWR on January 1st, 1922 but for the purposes of this album they are treated separately as there was little if any outward difference noticeable before the grouping took place one year later.

These eight constituents together with the Maryport & Carlisle Railway, Stratford-upon-Avon & Midland Junction Railway and the Wirral Railway plus several smaller concerns presented the newly formed LMS with well over 10,000 locomotives of a wide variety of design and age. It would perhaps be true to say that there were many excellent but ageing engines and relatively few that were modern and efficient.

With two historic rivals included in the LMS its early years were bound to be far from smooth. On the locomotive front Crewe was already far from happy with the outcome of the amalgamation with the LYR whereby George Hughes of the LYR became Chief Mechanical Engineer of the enlarged LNWR on the grounds of seniority. A second blow fell on Crewe after the grouping, although Hughes was chosen as CME of the new Company he was near retiring age, and in 1925 he was succeeded by Sir Henry Fowler who had been CME of the Midland since 1909. Fowler who had been quietly continuing the MR small engine policy at Derby immediately saw to the mass construction of his MR designs for use on most of the LMS system. Thus the three-cylinder compounds were soon to be found at work on the west coast main line, much to the dismay of Crewe. The products of Crewe were if anything mass produced and like all mass produced machinery they had a short life expectancy particularly when thrashed in the manner that was customary on the "Premier Line". Since there had been no new express engines designed since 1913 for the LNWR it was perhaps about time something new appeared on this route. However nothing could have been more calculated to cause resentment than the introduction of what was basically a 1905 MR design particularly after the unhappy experiences with the later Webb compounds.

Midland influence did not only apply to locomotives, new rolling stock was on the whole based on Midland designs, though when it came to sleeping and dining cars it was LNWR designs that were followed at first. The locomotive power class system of classifying engine power in relation to loads permitted was pure Midland. In 1928 the letters F for freight and P for passenger were added to the power class numbers and it is the post 1928 classes that I have used throughout this album. Lastly but by no means least the livery adopted by the LMS was Midland even to the large numerals on the locomotive tenders, all originally part of the MR train control system. At Crewe this did not work as tenders were never considered as married to one engine so it was sometimes possible to see an engine with a tender bearing another engine's number. After applying the crimson lake livery quite happily at first Crewe stopped repainting engines in LMS livery due, so it was said, to a reorganisation in the works, and many engines were returned to traffic after overhaul in LNWR black livery complete with their old numberplates. Even in later years after crimson lake had been dropped for all but the most important engines, "Claughton" 4-6-0s still continued to appear in black, though with the correct LMS number and insignia but with North Western lining out on the buffer beam!

George Hughes had, before his retirement, multiplied his LYR design of four-cylinder 4-6-0 for use on the west coast main line between Crewe and Carlisle. He also initiated the Horwich Mogul design which appeared in 1926 unhappily matched with a Fowler tender, the engine was pure Horwich and a fine machine at that. In Scotland the Glasgow & South Western stock was quickly displaced by MR types. Compounds appeared on the Caledonian whilst on the Highland section the only new engines to find a permanent home were the Horwich "Crabs". Of course, Fowler introduced some completely new classes, but these are not part of this album. With the appointment of William Stanier as CME in 1932 there emerged at last a true breed of LMS locomotive and the old differences began to fade. So did the pregrouping engines—the slaughter of the middle to late 1930s was rapid, so much so that when the LMS became part of

the nationalised British Railways in 1948 only a little over a third of the 1923 locomotive stock remained in traffic despite the intervention of World War II. This briefly then was the situation on the LMS in the years directly after its formation. Matters might have been worse and internally out of the public eye they possibly were.

In selecting the photographs for inclusion in LMS Album No 2 I have tried wherever possible to present a balanced selection, with if possible, pictures that included a little more than just a train. With the limitations of prewar photography this has been very difficult as the style of the time was the track-level three-quarter front view with little if anything else to distract the eye. I apologise if readers feel there are not enough Glasgow & South Western, North Staffordshire or Furness pictures, but these are very hard to come by. I have included building dates and withdrawal dates for most of the classes in the captions for those who it may interest, whilst I hope those who are not will bear with me.

Once again I must express my sincere thanks to the following photographers who have all given me complete freedom to use whatever I wished from their collections: F. R. Hebron, T. G. Hepburn, E. E. Smith, C. R. L. Coles, L. Hanson, J. G. Dewing, J. P. Wilson and A. B. MacLeod. Also to N. Fields for the pictures by the late R. D. Pollard and G. W. Smith as well as some of his own, to M. W. Earley for the pictures by the late J. Clarke, to E. A. Wilkinson of the LCGB for his help with pictures from the Ken Nunn Collection and lastly to G. M. Kichenside who has helped with negatives from the E. R. Wethersett and Locomotive Publishing Co. collections which are owned by the Publisher and for permitting me to browse through the Publisher's photographic files for the remaining photographs that complete this album. Final thanks go to my wife who, as usual, has put up with it all and whose helpful comments and criticisms have been invaluable.

August 1971   B.W.L.S.

Premier Line

In 1923 the LMS inherited slightly over 3,300 engines of London & North Western Railway origin. Pride of place amongst its express passenger locomotives was taken by the handsome Bowen-Cooke four-cylinder "Claughton" class 4-6-0s of which 130 examples were built at Crewe between 1913 and 1921. Un-named "Claughton" class 5P 4-6-0 No 5936 passes Tring with the 2.50 pm Euston-Manchester London Road express about 1931. The leading coach is an LYR brake composite. [*F. R. Hebron*

ABOVE: An unidentified oil-fired "Claughton" 4-6-0 is seen near Tamworth with a Manchester-Euston express in the late 1920s. Quite a number of LNWR express engines were equipped for oil burning during the unrest in the coal industry during the 1920s.
[*F. R. Hebron*

UPPER RIGHT: Bowen-Cooke "Claughton" 4-6-0 No 1407 *L./Cpl. J. A. Christie, V.C.,* later LMS No 5967, takes water from Bushey troughs with the down 1.30 pm "Midday Scot" on August 23, 1926. Despite the date the train has a strong North Western air about it with the locomotive and first three coaches still in LNWR livery.
[*F. R. Hebron*

RIGHT: Resplendent in the earliest form of LMS crimson lake livery unnamed "Claughton" 4-6-0 No 5944 takes water from Bushey troughs with the 11 am down Royal Train on August 15, 1925. The immaculately turned out LNWR Royal Train is formed of eight vehicles, the normal number when the King was travelling alone. The composition from the engine is brake 1st, 1st class sleeper, King's saloon, royal dining saloon, semi-royal saloon, 1st class dining saloon, 1st class sleeper and brake 1st.
[*F. R. Hebron*

ABOVE: The LMS rebuilt twenty "Claughtons" with larger boilers from 1928 and ten of them were also fitted with Beardmore-Caprotti valve gear. Two of the Caprotti engines, No 5908 *Alfred Fletcher* and No 5962 are seen climbing Camden bank with the 6.5 pm Manchester express about 1931.

[*F. R. Hebron*]

BELOW: "Claughton" 4-6-0 No 5929 *J. A. F. Aspinall* passes through Bushey and Oxhey station with the 10.30 am Euston-Liverpool Lime Street express about 1931. The leading coach, an elderly LNWR third, was probably added to the train at the last minute to ease overcrowding.

[*F. R. Hebron*]

LEFT: An unidentified "Claughton" 4-6-0 passes Willesden Junction with a down express freight in the late 1920s. With the introduction of the "Royal Scot" 4-6-0s the "Claughtons" soon found themselves demoted to lesser duties and withdrawal commenced in 1932 with all the un-rebuilt engines gone by the end of 1935. No 5977 had been scrapped in 1929 after the Doe Hill accident and two, Nos 5902 and 5971 were rebuilt as the prototypes of the "Patriot" class in 1930.   [T. G. Hepburn

BELOW: Some of the redundant "Claughtons" were transferred to the Midland section for which they were coupled with larger capacity tenders from withdrawn Robinson ROD 2-8-0s. No 6001, allocated to Nottingham, is seen at Derby in 1930 fitted with a Kylala single blastpipe and narrow ring piston valves in an attempt to reduce coal consumption, an experiment that was largely successful. However, repair costs were not decreased and the class was replaced by the large-scale introduction of "Patriot" and "Jubilee" 4-6-0s.   [T. G. Hepburn

RIGHT: Large boilered Caprotti "Claughton" class 5XP 4-6-0 No 5948 *Baltic,* allocated to Edge Hill, heads a Leeds-Manchester stopping train near Longwood in the mid 1930s. The reboilered "Claughtons" were fitted with smoke deflectors at the same time as the "Royal Scot" 4-6-0s after one of the latter class had been involved in an accident which had been caused by drifting smoke obscuring the driver's vision.　　　[*Cyril Whitaker*

BELOW: The last "Claughton" of all to remain in service was large boilered No 6004, formerly named *Princess Louise* until the "Princess Royal" class Pacific No 6204 appeared with the same name, is seen here passing Kilburn High Road with the 6.15 pm Camden-Birmingham goods on June 7, 1939. This was a regular turn at the time for this engine and No 6017 *Breadalbane,* both being allocated to Willesden. No 6004 was withdrawn in 1949, eight years after the previous "Claughton" withdrawals.　　　[*E. R. Wethersett*

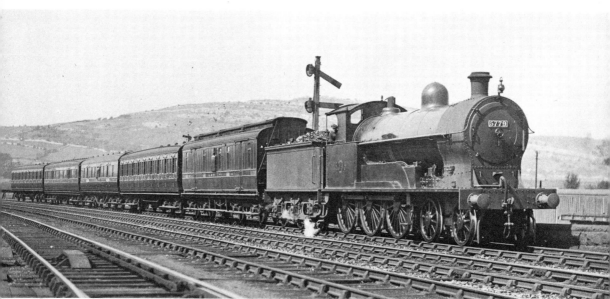

ABOVE: Bowen-Cooke "Prince of Wales" class 3P 4-6-0 No 25833 departs from Manchester London Road, now known as Piccadilly, with the 12 noon West of England express on June 1, 1936. The third and fourth vehicles are GWR through coaches. There were 244 "Prince of Wales" class engines built between 1911 and 1921 at Crewe, by the North British Locomotive Company and Beardmore. One further engine was built by Beardmore to LMS order in 1924.   [R. D. Pollard, courtesy N. Fields

UPPER LEFT: "Prince of Wales" class 4-6-0 No 25725 waits to leave Birmingham New Street with an express for Stafford and Crewe on the night of August 20, 1938. In common with several other pre-grouping classes the "Prince of Wales" 4-6-0s had 20,000 added to their numbers in 1934 so as to make room for the new standard classes then appearing.   [L. Hanson

LOWER LEFT: Several LNWR engines found their way onto the Furness section in the late 1920s and "Prince of Wales" 4-6-0 No 5779 is seen approaching Carnforth with the 3.20 pm stopping train from Barrow-in-Furness in May 1928.   [F. R. Hebron

ABOVE: Bowen-Cooke "Prince of Wales" class 3P 4-6-0 No 5765, fitted with a Belpaire firebox, and a Whale "Experiment" class 3P 4-6-0 double-head a northbound goods away from Carnforth in May 1928. The "Prince of Wales" 4-6-0s were a superheated version of George Whale's "Experiment" class introduced in 1905. [*F. R. Hebron*

LEFT: Whale "Experiment" class 3P 4-6-0 No 5464 *City of Glasgow* leaves Willesden Junction with an up parcels train on July 27, 1930. Scrapping of the 105 "Experiments" started in 1925 and all were gone by the end of 1935.

[*E. R. Wethersett*

RIGHT: A grimy unidentified Whale "19in goods" class 4F 4-6-0 passes under the road bridge at the south end of Cambridge station as it leaves with the 11.14 am train for Bletchley in June 1936. The rear of the old LNWR engine shed can just be seen on the extreme left. [*J. G. Dewing*

BELOW: Whale "19in goods" 4-6-0 No 8852 takes water from Dillicar troughs in the beautiful Lune Gorge with a down express freight about 1931. There were 170 of these engines built between 1906 and 1909. Three survived to nationalisation and No 8824, built in 1908, was the last LNWR 4-6-0 when withdrawn in 1950 barely outliving the last "Prince of Wales" 4-6-0.   [*F. R. Hebron*

ABOVE: Rebuilt "Precursor" class 4-4-0 No 2579 *Ganymede,* later LMS No 5231, leaves Derby with an express for Crewe in 1925. Designed by George Whale, 130 "Precursors" were built at Crewe between 1904 and 1907. From 1913 onwards 68 were rebuilt with superheaters and piston valves (excluding No 5270 *Marmion* which retained slide valves) and were almost identical with the "George the Fifth" class. [*T. G. Hepburn*

UPPER LEFT: Bowen-Cooke "George the Fifth" class 4-4-0 No 882 *Canada,* later LMS No 5351, takes water from Bushey troughs with a Fleetwood-Euston boat train on July 31, 1926. The "Georges" were a superheated development of George Whale's "Precursor" class of 1904 and 90 were built at Crewe between 1910 and 1915. [*F. R. Hebron*

LOWER LEFT: "George the Fifth" class 3P 4-4-0 No 5371 *Moorhen,* fitted with a Weir feed-water heater, passes Berkhamsted with an East Lancashire-Euston express in 1927. The last three "George the Fifth" 4-4-0s were withdrawn in 1948 with No 5351, formerly named *India,* being the last. The six coaches behind the leading LNWR brake composite are all of the earliest style of LMS corridor coach with two windows per seating bay. All six appear to be all steel open thirds. [*F. R. Hebron*

ABOVE: Rebuilt "Precursor" class 3P 4-4-0 No 5308 *Simoon* passes Tring with an up Birmingham "two hour" express about 1931. The third coach is one of the magnificent LNWR twelve-wheel clerestory dining cars of the style first introduced in 1894.
[*F. R. Hebron*

BELOW: Another rebuilt "Precursor" 4-4-0 No 5310 *Thunderer* climbs Camden bank with the 4 pm Euston-Manchester London Road express about 1931. Both these engines are painted in the post 1927 black livery and retain their round topped fireboxes.
[*F. R. Hebron*

RIGHT: Rebuilt "Precursor" 4-4-0 No 5308 *Simoom* and "Claughton" No 6016 head the 6.5 pm Euston-Manchester express near Kenton in April 1928. The second coach is an LNWR family saloon.   [*F. R. Hebron*

RIGHT: F. W. Webb "Precedent" class 1P 2-4-0 No 5069 *Penrith Beacon* struggles past Hest Bank troughs in 1927 with a northbound excursion after the train engine, a "Claughton", had failed.
[*F. R. Hebron*]

BELOW: Webb "Waterloo" class 1P 2-4-0 No 5104 *Woodlark* departs from Carlisle Citadel with the 4.25 pm stopping train for Penrith in 1931. Both the 6ft 9in "Precedent" and 6ft 3in "Waterloo" classes were known collectively as "Jumbos" on the LNWR. There were 166 of the former and 90 of the latter built but only 80 and 30 respectively came into LMS ownership and the last went in 1936.
[*F. R. Hebron*]

LEFT: Webb "Waterloo" class 2-4-0 No 124 *Marquis Douro,* allocated LMS No 5090, heads a down Engineer's Dept train past Hatch End on August 23, 1926. It was probably deputising for *Engineer Watford* seen below.

[*F. R. Hebron*

BELOW: In 1923-4 five "Waterloo" class 2-4-0s were transferred to the Engineer's Dept for working permanent way trains. They were given the names of the depots to which they were attached and *Engineer Watford,* formerly LNWR No 793 *Martin* which was allocated LMS No 5101, is seen at Watford shed on August 5, 1935. At the grouping there were already three "Waterloo" and two "Samson" class 2-4-0s attached to the Engineer's Dept. [*E. R. Wethersett*

RIGHT: Webb "Precedent" class 1P 2-4-0 No 5000 *Princess Beatrice* leaves Nottingham London Road low level station with a train for Northampton via the GN & LNW Joint line in 1930. The three coaches are of LYR origin. [*T. G. Hepburn*

BELOW: Webb "Cauliflower" class 2F 0-6-0 No 8367 enters Fenny Stratford with a Cambridge-Bletchley train, summer 1938. The leading coach is one of the celebrated Clayton MR clerestories, in this case a non-corridor compartment third. The remaining coaches are all Stanier LMS flush sided steel panelled corridor stock which became the hallmark of the LMS in later years. [*C. R. L. Coles*

ABOVE: Webb "17in Coal Engine" class 2F 0-6-0 No 8204 trundles a down local freight through Shrewsbury station, summer 1937. There were 500 of these engines built between 1873 and 1892 of which 227 came into the LMS who passed 46 on to British Railways in 1948.

[E. E. Smith]

BELOW: Webb "Cauliflower" class 2F 0-6-0 No 8529 shunts empty stock at the Wolverhampton end of Birmingham New Street on May 7, 1938. All but two of the 310 engines built of this class in the years 1880-1902 came into LMS stock and 69 survived nationalisation.

[L. Hanson]

ABOVE: Bowen-Cooke "G1" class 6F 0-8-0 No 9196 heads an up goods at Wreay on December 23, 1938. The train includes ten new private owner wagons being delivered from their makers. This engine was built as a "G1" in 1912 but many "G1s" were rebuilt from earlier Webb and Whale 0-8-0s. *[E. E. Smith*

UPPER LEFT: "G2a" class 7F 0-8-0 No 9200 meets sister engine No 9299 heading a down freight out of Northchurch tunnel, north of Berkhamsted on June 17, 1947. The "G2a" class 7F engines were further rebuilds of the "G1" class engines with 175lb sq/in boilers in place of their original 160lb sq/in ones, thus bringing them into line with the "G2" class introduced by H. P. M. Beames in 1921. *[E. R. Wethersett*

LOWER LEFT: "G1" class 6F 0-8-0 No 9105, still fitted with a round topped firebox and coupled with a Webb tender previously used behind No 9052, stands outside Willesden shed on September 17, 1932. In 1948 there were 123 "G1", 60 "G2" and 273 "G2a" engines included in BR stock. *[E. R. Wethersett*

ABOVE: "G1" class 6F 0-8-0 No 8908 runs beside the Oxford Canal at Brinklow with a northbound cattle train in 1937. No 8908 began life as a Webb "B" class four-cylinder compound and was converted to a "G1" class simple in the mid 1920s.

[T. G. Hepburn]

BELOW: Bowen-Cooke class 6F 0-8-2T No 7877 leaves Edge Hill sorting sidings with a transfer freight for Garston Dock in the late 1930s. Thirty examples of this heavy tank version of the "G" class 0-8-0 were built between 1911 and 1917.

[Eric Treacy]

UPPER LEFT: Bowen-Cooke "Prince of Wales Tank" class 4P 4-6-2T No 6959, painted in plain black livery but with the LMS coat of arms on the bunker sides, nears Carnforth with a Carlisle-Preston stopping train in May 1928. There were 47 of these superheated Pacific tanks built between 1910 and 1916.   [F. R. Hebron

LOWER LEFT: Another "Prince of Wales Tank", No 6978 couples onto a passenger train at the Birmingham end of Coventry station on April 23, 1935. The first of these engines was withdrawn the following year and all had gone by the end of 1941.   [L. Hanson

BELOW: Whale "Precursor Tank" class 2P 4-4-2T No 6813 storms out of Carlisle as pilot to an unidentified Hughes LYR "N1" class 5P 4-6-0 with an up express for Manchester in 1931. Built between 1906 and 1909, many of the 50 "Precursor Tanks" were used on outer suburban trains from Euston. Scrapping commenced in 1927 and the last went in 1940.   [F. R. Hebron

ABOVE: One of the Watford based Whale "Precursor Tanks", No 6794 heads a Watford-Bletchley local near King's Langley on September 7, 1929. The train is formed of five standard LMS non-corridor coaches of the style built in the late 1920s.
[E. R. Wethersett

LEFT: One of the last surviving Webb 4ft 6in class 1P 2-4-2Ts, No 6526 heads the one coach branch train away from Stanmore on July 11, 1931. There were 88 of these engines built between 1882 and 1890 and four were sold to the Wirral Railway in 1913. These four and all but two of the remaining LNWR engines came into LMS ownership and the class became extinct in 1932.
[E. R. Wethersett

RIGHT: Webb 5ft "Watford" class 2P 0-6-2T No 6871 takes water at Watford Junction in the mid 1930s. Built between 1898 and 1902 these engines were used on the Euston and Broad Street to Watford local trains before electrification was completed in 1922. Two survived nationalisation and were withdrawn in 1953. [*C. R. L. Coles*

BELOW: A Webb 4ft 3in "Coal Tank" class 2F 0-6-2T heads a Bangor-Llandudno Junction push-pull train near Penmaenmawr about 1933. 300 of these "Coal Tanks" were built in the years 1881-96 and all but nine came into LMS stock. No 7799, built in 1888, was the last LNWR tank engine when withdrawn in 1958 and it is now preserved at Penrhyn Castle. [*F. R. Hebron*

UPPER LEFT: Webb "Coal Tank" class 2F 0-6-2T No 7720 leaves Robert Stephenson's Britannia Tubular Bridge over the Menai Straits with a Bangor-Holyhead stopping train about 1933. The Britannia Tubular Bridge, which was built in 1850, was badly damaged by fire on the night of May 23, 1970. When completely repaired it will be a very different bridge with only the original masonry piers remaining. [F. R. Hebron

LOWER LEFT: Webb 5ft 6in class 1P 2-4-2T No 6624 passes Kinnerton with a Denbigh-Chester fast train about 1930. Of the 160 Webb 5ft 6in 2-4-2Ts built between 1890 and 1897, three were scrapped before the grouping and 43 survived to 1948, the last being withdrawn in 1955. [Locomotive Publishing Co.

UPPER RIGHT: A Llandudno Junction-Bangor push pull train formed of LNWR stock nears Penmaenmawr propelled by a Webb "Coal Tank" about 1933. It is strange that these engines, many of which were push pull fitted, were always in the freight power class series.
[F. R. Hebron

LOWER RIGHT: Another push pull fitted Webb "Coal Tank" class 2F 0-6-2T, No 7769 leaves Stanbridgeford with a Luton-Leighton Buzzard train in the late 1930s.
[W. S. Garth

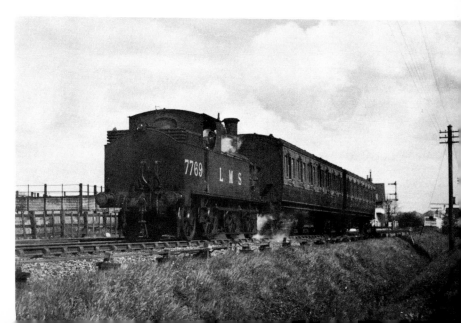

Ramsbottom 0-4-0ST No 3033, later LMS No 7207, stands with the Willesden breakdown train on August 21, 1926. It was from a class of 17 introduced in 1864, one of which was sold before the grouping and survived to be preserved by BR in 1954.

[*F. R. Hebron*

Ramsbottom "Special Tank" class 2F 0-6-0ST Carriage Dept. No 8 *Earlestown* is seen inside Crewe works on July 3, 1938 after having been overhauled. *Earlestown* was one of six engines of this class allocated to the Carriage Dept for shunting at Wolverton works. There were originally 258 engines in the class but only five of the Carriage Dept locos and one other allocated to Crewe works survived to come into BR ownership. The last was scrapped in 1959.

[*Neville Fields*

Whale class 2F 0-6-0ST No 27477 stands outside Crewe South shed on May 1, 1938. There were 45 of these square-tanked 0-6-0STs which were rebuilt from Webb "17in Coal Engines" between 1905 and 1907 and the last example was withdrawn in 1948.

[*J. G. Dewing*

Midland

Veteran Kirtley double framed class 1P 2-4-0 No 20012 heads a Cambridge-Kettering train near Cranford in 1937. Like so many of the 2,925 Midland engines included in LMS stock, it has received various alterations in the course of time. It has been fitted with a Johnson boiler, cab and tender, whilst Deeley supplied the chimney and smokebox door. It was this last feature that was to spoil the appearance of all the graceful Johnson engines in later years and it remained standard for the MR and LMS until Stanier appeared on the scene. Twenty-nine of these robust engines were built between 1866 and 1874 and the last, No 20002, was withdrawn for preservation in 1947. *[T. G. Hepburn*

ABOVE: Kirtley double framed class 1P 0-4-4T No 1219, fitted with condensing apparatus for working through the Metropolitan tunnels to Moorgate, is seen beside the old coaling stage at Kentish Town shed on September 2, 1933. There were 26 of these condensing tanks built in 1869-70. All of them came into the LMS and the last was withdrawn in 1935. Like most of the Kirtley engines they were rebuilt in various ways by Johnson and Deeley.
[*E. R. Wethersett*

UPPER RIGHT: Kirtley double framed class 1F 0-6-0 No 2650 and standard Fowler LMS built class 4F 0-6-0 No 4243 double head an up goods past Derby station in the late 1920s. Large numbers of these engines were built between 1863 and 1874 and 449 were included in LMS stock. 80 of them had served with the ROD mainly in France and Belgium during World War I. Four survived in 1948, and the last was withdrawn by BR in 1951.
[*T. G. Hepburn*

LOWER RIGHT: Many of the Kirtley class 1F 0-6-0s were rebuilt with Deeley boilers, Belpaire fireboxes and larger cylinders. Some like No 2858, seen leaving Milford Tunnel near Duffield with an up goods about 1930, also received larger Deeley cabs in place of the Johnson version earlier fitted. These rebuilt engines were classed 2F.
[*F. R. Hebron*

The most numerous class of Johnson 2-4-0 was the 6ft 9in version of which 65 were built between 1876 and 1881. Class 1P No 207 has just passed Coldham Junction as it approaches Cambridge with a train from Kettering on August 3, 1934.

[*E. R. Wethersett*

Johnson class 1P 6ft 9in 2-4-0 No 254, still retaining its original boiler, has steam to spare as it climbs the Lickey incline with an inspection saloon in 1935.

[*F. R. Hebron*

RIGHT: The earliest Johnson 4-4-0s were the 6ft 6in and 7ft versions built in 1876 and 1877 respectively. Class 1P 7ft 4-4-0 No 325 is seen at Nottingham in the mid 1920s. They were never rebuilt like the later engines and the last survivor was scrapped in 1934.
[T. G. Hepburn

ABOVE: Resplendent in LMS crimson lake, Johnson class 1P 7ft 6½in 4-2-2 No 641 stands in Nottingham Midland at the head of a St Pancras express in 1926. Of the 85 Johnson singles built between 1887 and 1900, 43 survived in 1923 and all were gone by the end of 1928. The last, No 673 has been preserved as MR No 118. [T. G. Hepburn

RIGHT: Johnson class 1P 6ft 9in 2-4-0 No 20251, fitted with a Belpaire firebox, stands in Bedford station in June 1939. The last of these engines, No 20216 was withdrawn in 1948.
[C. R. L. Coles

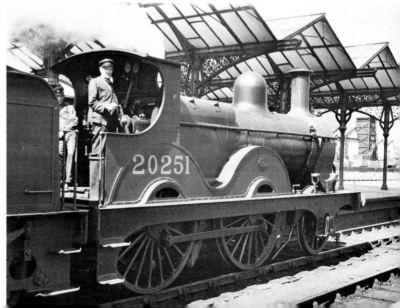

Rebuilt Johnson class 2P 6ft 6in 4-4-0 No 435 leaves Peterborough East with the 5.10 pm stopping train for Leicester on September 12, 1926. Allocated to Saltley depot Birmingham, No 435 was withdrawn the following year. It was one of 55 built between 1893 and 1900 and were subsequently rebuilt by Richard Deeley from 1905. From 1914 onwards 35 (excluding No 435) were further rebuilt by Henry Fowler with superheated boilers and 7ft diameter driving wheels so as to conform with his "483" class 2P engines which themselves were rebuilds of earlier Johnson 4-4-0s introduced in 1882. Many of these were believed to be accountancy rebuilds where little if any of the original engine remained, a clever way of getting round the royalty demands from the Schmidt superheater company who charged a higher royalty for superheaters fitted to new engines. [*F. R. Hebron*

Another later Deeley rebuild, Johnson class 2P 6ft 9in 4-4-0 No 338, fitted with a Belpaire firebox and extended smokebox but not superheated, is seen leaving New Mills with a Manchester Central-Hope train on August 4, 1935. There were 30 of these engines built in 1882-83 and all survived to 1923 when five were rebuilt to the "483" class. The others were all scrapped between 1925 and 1937.

[R. D. Pollard, courtesy N. Fields

ABOVE: Rebuilt Johnson class 3P 4-4-0 No 759 pilots "483" class 2P 4-4-0 No 530 with a Manchester-Derby express near Whatstandwell about 1930. All but five of the 80 class 3P 4-4-0s built between 1900 and 1905 were fitted with super-heaters and larger cylinders by Henry Fowler from 1913 onwards. Note the use of bogie brakes on both engines.

[*Locomotive Publishing Co.*

RIGHT: Class 3P 4-4-0 No 762 enters Kettering with a stopping train from North-ampton in June 1939. Withdrawal of the last superheated class 3P took place in 1952 but the five un-rebuilt engines had all gone by the end of 1926.

[*C. R. L. Coles*

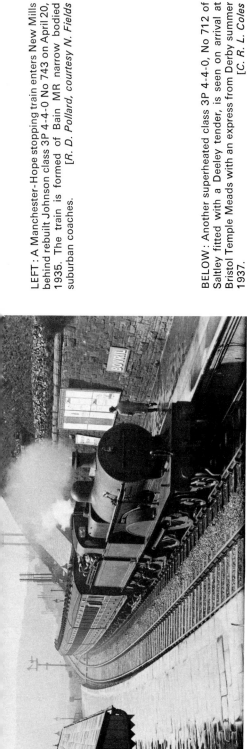

LEFT: A Manchester-Hope stopping train enters New Mills behind rebuilt Johnson class 3P 4-4-0 No 743 on April 20, 1935. The train is formed of Bain MR narrow bodied suburban coaches. [R. D. Pollard, courtesy N. Fields

BELOW: Another superheated class 3P 4-4-0, No 712 of Saltley fitted with a Deeley tender, is seen on arrival at Bristol Temple Meads with an express from Derby summer 1937. [C. R. L. Coles

ABOVE: Rebuilt Johnson class 2P 4-4-0 No 391 leaves Grange-over-Sands with a Barrow-in-Furness-Carnforth stopping train in May 1928. No 391, allocated to Carlisle Upperby North Western shed, was one of fifteen 6ft 6in 4-4-0s built in 1888 and has been rebuilt by Deeley and Fowler with a Belpaire firebox and extended smokebox. This class was to remain saturated and the last engine was not scrapped until 1952.

[*F. R. Hebron*]

BELOW: Fowler "483" class 2P rebuilt 7ft 4-4-0 No 461 leaves Elstree Tunnel in 1925 with the 2.45 pm St Pancras-Nottingham express. The first two vehicles, a six-wheel corridor full brake and a bogie brake third, are of LNWR origin. The "483" class introduced in 1912 was the final development of the Midland class 2 4-4-0 all of which were nominally rebuilds of earlier Johnson engines most of which had had an intermediate rebuild by Deeley.

[F. R. Hebron

LEFT: Fowler "483" class 2P 4-4-0 No 554 pilots an unidentified compound with the up "Thames Forth" express seen heading out of Nottingham towards Edwalton in the mid 1930s.

[*T. G. Hepburn*

BELOW: An oil burning "483" class 2P 4-4-0 No 555 passes Mill Hill with a St Pancras-Bedford fast train on August 27, 1926. Many Midland engines were equipped for oil burning from 1921.

[*F. R. Hebron*

RIGHT: One of the five 6ft 9in class 2P 4-4-0s rebuilt to the "483" class in 1923, No 332 fitted with an exhaust steam injector, leaves New Mills with a Chinley-Marple local on June 25, 1938.
[R. D. Pollard, courtesy N. Fields

BELOW: A Manchester Central-Buxton fast train passes Chapel-en-le-Frith on May 18, 1937 behind "483" class 2P 4-4-0 No 412 of Buxton shed.
[R. D. Pollard, courtesy N. Fields

The up "Thames Clyde" express departs from Carlisle Citadel hauled by Fowler "483" class 2P 4-4-0 No. 436, bearing a Carlisle Durranhill shed plate, piloting the pioneer Bowen-Cooke LNWR "Claughton" class 5P four-cylinder 4-6-0 No 5900 *Sir Gilbert Claughton* in 1931. On the adjacent track an LNER class D20 4-4-0 No 2028 waits patiently to back onto its train for Newcastle whilst further to the left a Hughes LYR "N1" class 5P 4-6-0 can be seen marshalling stock. In 1928 Sir Henry Fowler introduced a 6ft 9in version of the "483" class and 138 examples were built.   [*F. R. Hebron*

UPPER LEFT: Deeley class 4P three-cylinder compound 4-4-0 No 1031 approaches Elstree about 1930 with an express from Leeds due to arrive at St Pancras at 4.2 pm. The leading coach is a Clayton twelve-wheel dining car. Introduced in 1905 the Deeley compounds were a development of the Smith/Johnson engines of 1901. Forty were built and the five earlier engines were rebuilt to conform. Later they were all superheated by Fowler.

[*F. R. Hebron*

LOWER LEFT: Deeley three-cylinder compound No 1030 is seen at Kentish Town shed in 1926. Although fitted with an extended smokebox the engine remains saturated. Superheating of all 45 engines was completed the following year. [*F. R. Hebron*

ABOVE: A compound in decline, No 1021 heads away from Romiley with a three coach Manchester-Chinley local on May 4, 1935. Scrapping of the compounds started in 1948 and the last MR built engine went in 1953. [*R. D. Pollard, courtesy N. Fields*

ABOVE: Deeley class 4P three-cylinder compound 7ft 4-4-0 No 1012, allocated to Leeds Holbeck shed, passes Duffield with a Sheffield-Bristol express about 1930. Again we see one of the celebrated Clayton clerestory dining cars next to the engine.   [Locomotive Publishing Co.

BELOW: Between 1924 and 1932 the LMS built a further 195 three-cylinder compounds with 6ft 9in diameter driving wheels. One of these, No 1048 hurries a St Pancras-Leeds express down the 1 in 200 at Edwalton on the Nottingham outskirts in the mid 1930s. [T. G. Hepburn

ABOVE: Deeley class 3F 5ft 3in 0-6-0 No 3815 passes the MSJA platforms at Manchester London Road with a local pick-up freight on April 5, 1938. Many of the class 2F 0-6-0s of both varieties were rebuilt by Johnson and Deeley to class 3F. Engines numbered above 3764 were built new as class 3F. The total number of all the Johnson and Deeley 0-6-0s built between 1875 and 1908 was 935, all of which came into LMS ownership.

[R. D. Pollard, courtesy N. Fields

UPPER LEFT: Rebuilt Johnson class 2F 4ft 11in 0-6-0 No 22930 has just joined the main line from St Pancras at Kettering Junction with a train from Cambridge in June 1939. There were two types of Johnson 0-6-0 built from 1875 onwards, the first with 4ft 11in diameter driving wheels and the other with 5ft 3in. No 22930 was one of many rebuilt by Deeley with a Belpaire firebox and larger cab.

[C. R. L. Coles

LOWER LEFT: Johnson class 2F 5ft 3in 0-6-0 No 3477, remaining basically in its original condition, approaches Mill Hill with an up pick-up goods on August 27, 1926. Today the M1 motorway runs parallel to the railway at this point almost next to the up slow line.

[F. R. Hebron

ABOVE: Johnson class 2F 5ft 3in 0-6-0 No 3042, fitted with a Belpaire firebox and Deeley cab, and class 1P 6ft 9in 2-4-0 No 20216 stand outside Kettering shed on a June afternoon in 1939.　　　[C. R. L. Coles

BELOW: A pair of Deeley class 3F 5ft 3in 0-6-0 rebuilds, with No. 3763 leading, climb away from London Road Junction, Nottingham with a heavy coal train bound for Brent in the early 1930s.　　　[T. G. Hepburn

ABOVE: Fowler class 4F 0-6-0 No 3927 climbs past Gow Hole sidings on the slow line with a summer Saturday Llandudno-Sheffield train on August 12, 1939. An LYR brake composite is next to the engine. The Fowler class 4F 0-6-0 was the final development of the Johnson 0-6-0 of 1875 and was introduced in 1911. The MR built 192 up to 1922.   [R. D. Pollard, courtesy N. Fields

LEFT: Fowler class 4F 0-6-0 No 3881 rattles downgrade towards New Mills South Junction with a down goods on July 2, 1938. Gow Hole sidings can be seen in the background. The Fowler 4F was chosen for mass production by the LMS in 1924 and 575 had been built by the time the last appeared in 1941.

[R. D. Pollard, courtesy N. Fields

ABOVE: Johnson class 1P 5ft 7in 0-4-4T No 1252 approaches Nottingham Midland with a local from Newark about 1930. There were 205 Johnson 0-4-4Ts built between 1875 and 1900, 30 with 5ft 7in diameter driving wheels whilst all the rest had 5ft 4in drivers. The first of these tanks was withdrawn in 1919 but it was not until 1960 that the last disappeared. [T. G. Hepburn

RIGHT: Begrimed Johnson class 1P 5ft 4in 0-4-4T No 1287, fitted with a Belpaire firebox, approaches Upminster with the push pull train from Romford on September 24, 1947. The electrified track is that over which the LT District Line trains run.

[E. R. Wethersett

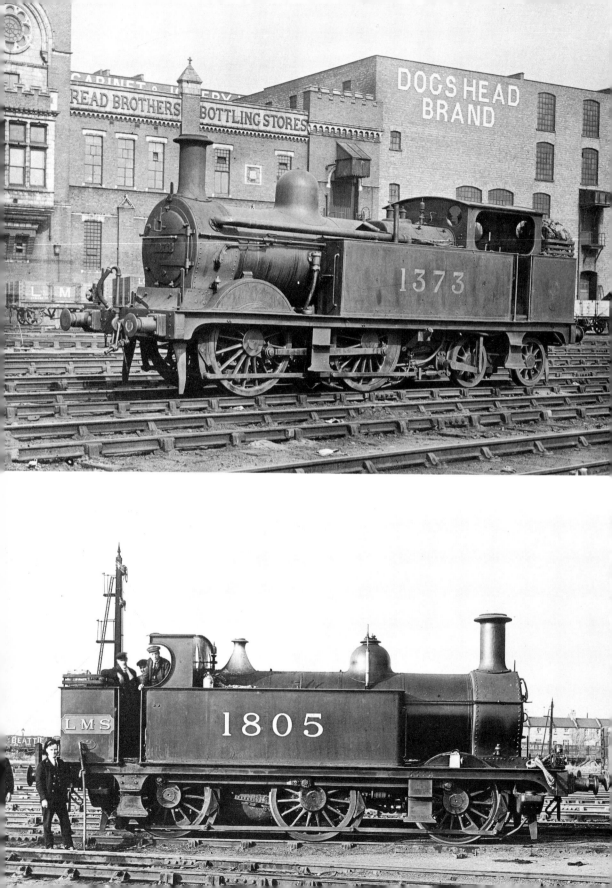

UPPER LEFT: One of the 26 Johnson class 1P 5ft 4in 0-4-4Ts fitted with condensing apparatus for working over the Metropolitan widened lines poses in front of the Read Brothers bottling store adjacent to Kentish Town shed—a favourite location over the years for portraits of Midland locomotives. No 1373 was photographed on September 4, 1926 in the full crimson lake livery with the LMS coat of arms on the bunker sides.   [F. R. Hebron

LOWER LEFT: Johnson class 1F 0-6-0T No 1805 built in 1891 pauses during shunting in the late 1920s. It is in the pre 1928 plain black freight engine livery with the vermillion backed LMS panel on the bunker sides. Introduced in 1874 the class eventually totalled 280 examples. The last five were not withdrawn officially until Christmas Day 1966 when a 100 year agreement made by the Midland Railway for shunting at the Staveley ironworks came to an end.
                                    [Locomotive Publishing Co.

ABOVE: One of the ten small Deeley 0-4-0Ts, No 1535 is seen inside Derby Works on July 11, 1937 during an overhaul. Introduced in 1907 two of these engines also survived to the end of 1966 for shunting at the Staveley ironworks.
                                    [L. Hanson

ABOVE: Deeley class 3P 0-6-4T No 2013 departs from St Pancras with the 5.10 pm St Albans train formed of Bain MR wide bodied suburban coaches on September 4, 1926. There were 40 "Flatirons" built in 1907 and despite superheating they remained poor engines. After several derailments due to poor riding they were withdrawn between 1935 and 1938.

[F. R. Hebron]

BELOW: The famous four-cylinder 0-10-0 Lickey banker No 2290 designed by Sir Henry Fowler and built at Derby in 1919 is seen shortly before the grouping when equipped for burning oil. Several other engines were tried on banking duties up the Lickey Incline but "Big Bertha" carried on until replaced by a BR standard class 9F 2-10-0 in 1956.

[Locomotive Publishing Co.

Lancashire & Yorkshire

UPPER LEFT: An unidentified Hughes "N1" class 5P four-cylinder 4-6-0 enters Sheffield Victoria with the 5 pm Bradford Exchange-Marylebone express formed of LNER stock in the mid 1930s.   [T. G. Hepburn

LOWER LEFT: One of the LMS built Hughes class 5P 4-6-0s, No 10465 passes Oxenholme with a Manchester-Glasgow express about 1930. This was one of twenty originally intended as 4-6-4Ts but which were turned out as 4-6-0s in 1924/5.   [F. R. Hebron

UPPER RIGHT: Still in LYR livery No 1518, later LMS No 10419 and the last of fifteen "N1" class engines rebuilt from earlier Hughes 4-6-0s, waits to leave York with a Newcastle-Liverpool express at 7 pm on June 27, 1925.   [F. R. Hebron

LOWER RIGHT: Hughes "P1" class 5P 4-6-4T No 11110 runs light out of Manchester Victoria on April 8, 1939. Only ten of this tank version of the Hughes 4-6-0 were built in 1924 and all were withdrawn between 1938 and 1942.   [J. P. Wilson

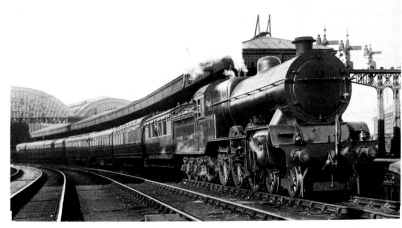

BELOW: Hughes "N1" class 5P four-cylinder 4-6-0 No 10431 departs from York with a lightweight express about 1930. There were eventually a total of 70 of these engines. Many suffered a premature withdrawal from 1934 onwards but seven lasted into BR days and the last, No 10455, went in 1951. [Locomotive Publishing Co.

UPPER RIGHT: Aspinall "L1" class 2P 4-4-2 No 10303 passes Middleton Junction with a Liverpool-Bradford express in 1924. Forty of these "Highflyers" were built between 1899 and 1902 and they were scrapped between 1926 and 1934.
[G. W. Smith, courtesy N. Fields

LOWER RIGHT: Another Aspinall "Highflyer" class 2P 4-4-2, No 10320 of Low Moor shed, is seen in the engine siding at Nottingham carriage sidings after arriving with a Bradford-St Pancras express in 1929. Note the door in the cab front—an unusual feature of these the only Atlantic tender engines to come into the LMS. [T. G. Hepburn

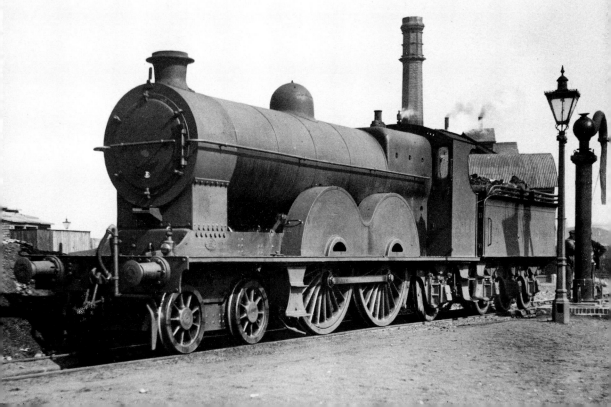

ABOVE: Hughes "Q4" class 7F 0-8-0 No 12857 takes water from Luddendenfoot troughs as it heads east over the Calder Valley main line with a train of coal empties on September 7, 1945. This class introduced in 1912 eventually totalled 150 engines, several had been rebuilt from Aspinall "Q1" and Hughes "Q3" classes.

[E. R. Wethersett

RIGHT: One of the earlier Hughes 0-8-0s, "Q3" class 6F No 12834 awaits its next duty inside Wigan Wallgate shed on May 2, 1948. Appropriately nicknamed "Teddy Bears" there were 69 in the class introduced in 1910, 29 had been rebuilt from the Aspinall "Q1" class and together with the "Q4" version they became extinct in 1951. How we would like to see a set of Daily Engine Arrangements such as must have been set out on the board to the left again!

[J. G. Dewing

ABOVE: Aspinall "F19" class 2F 0-6-0 No 12345 heads a long east-bound train of coal empties over the Calder Valley main line near Mytholmroyd on August 8, 1947. This class was the most numerous on the LYR with 448 examples built between 1889 and 1917.

[E. R. Wethersett

BELOW: On the same day 0-6-0 No 12574, a Hughes "F22" class 3F rebuild of the Aspinall "F19", heads a Sowerby Bridge-Todmorden local away from Mytholmroyd. Between 1913 and 1922 a total of 63 of these rebuilds appeared and were identical with the 20 built new in 1912.

[E. R. Wethersett

LEFT: Aspinall "K2" class 2P 2-4-2T No 10732 leaves Moston with a Manchester-Bury stopping train formed of LYR stock about 1925. There were 309 of these versatile radial tanks built between 1889 and 1910.

[*G. W. Smith, courtesy N. Fields*

RIGHT: Aspinall class 2P 2-4-2T No 10767 makes an unusual sight as it takes water from Lea Road troughs with the 3.45 pm Preston-Blackpool slow on May 4, 1936. The leading coach is of Stanier LMS design whilst the remainder appear to be LYR. Scrapping of the radial tanks started in 1927 and the last did not go until 1961. George Hughes brought out a superheated version in 1911 of which 20 were built and 44 of the Aspinall engines were rebuilt to conform.

[*E. R. Wethersett*

LEFT: Aspinall radial tank No 10887 stands in Lockwood station with a Huddersfield-Clayton West train on May 21, 1949. This engine has been rebuilt with a Belpaire firebox and extended smokebox.

[*Neville Fields*

RIGHT: Aspinall "B7" class 0-4-0ST No 11235 slumbers inside Burton-on-Trent shed about 1935. The "Pugs" were the smallest engines amongst the 1,721 of LYR design included in LMS stock. There were 57 built between 1891 and 1910 and they were used mainly in the Liverpool docks but in LMS days and after they were sent to many places far removed from their native counties. [*E. E. Smith*

BELOW: Aspinall "Pug" No 11217 is seen inside Derby roundhouse on October 16, 1938. Sister engine No 11218 was the last surviving LYR engine when withdrawn late in 1964, and it is now preserved together with No 11234 on the K & WVR. [*L. Hanson*

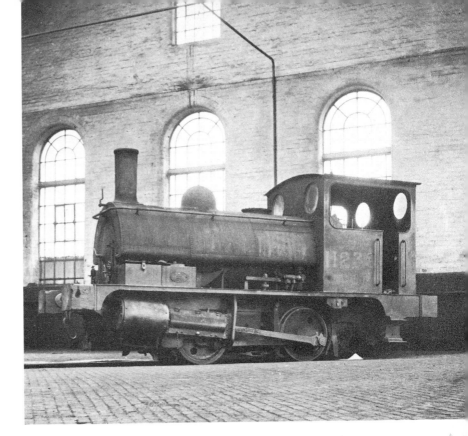

Furness

UPPER RIGHT: Pettigrew class 1P 6ft 6in 4-4-0 No. 10144 leaves Carlisle Citadel with a Maryport train in 1931. There were four of these engines built in 1900-1 and they were withdrawn in 1930-1. *[F. R. Hebron*

LOWER RIGHT: Largest amongst the 136 engines inherited by the LMS from the Furness Railway were the five Rutherford Baltic tanks built in 1921. Here class 4P 4-6-4T No 11104 passes Hest Bank with a Barrow-in-Furness-Lancaster train in 1927. They were scrapped between 1934 and 1940. *[F. R. Hebron*

BELOW: Pettigrew class 2F 4ft 8in 0-6-0 No 12471 pulls slowly away from Carnforth with a goods train for Barrow-in-Furness in May 1928. There were sixteen engines included in this class, twelve having 4ft 8in diameter driving wheels and the remaining four having 5ft 1in drivers. They were built between 1899 and 1907 and all were withdrawn by the end of 1936. *[F. R. Hebron*

London Tilbury & Southend

ABOVE: There were 94 engines of LTSR origin included in Midland Railway stock at the grouping. Seventy Atlantic tanks were amongst them and we see Thomas Whitelegg class 2P 4-4-2T No 2175, formerly LTSR No 68 *Mark Lane*, leaving Mill Hill with the 4 pm St Pancras-St Albans train on July 13, 1926. This class consisted of 18 engines built between 1900 and 1903 and all but one survived to nationalisation, the last being scrapped in 1953.   [*F. R. Hebron*

UPPER RIGHT: T. Whitelegg class 3P 4-4-2T No 2147, previously LMS No 2176 and LTSR No 79 *Rippleside*, nears Hornchurch with the Ealing-Southend through train in the mid 1930s. The coaches used on this service were the only corridor vehicles owned by the LTSR. The service ceased with the outbreak of World War II and was never restored. No 2176, sister to the preserved No 80 *Thundersley*, was one of four engines built in 1909. They were the final development of Whitelegg's 4-4-2Ts and twelve older engines were rebuilt to the same design. Also a further 35 were built by the LMS (see next page) in the years 1923-1930.   [*F. R. Hebron*

LOWER RIGHT: One of Robert Whitelegg's class 3P 4-6-4Ts, No 2104 still in MR livery, waits to leave St Pancras in 1924 with the 5.25 pm St Albans train. This class totalled eight engines built in 1912 the year the LTSR was taken over by the Midland. They were all scrapped between 1929 and 1934.   [*F. R. Hebron*

UPPER LEFT: One of the 35 LMS built T. Whitelegg class 3P 4-4-2Ts, No 2134 built in 1927, leaves Southend East with a Fenchurch Street via Tilbury train on August 21, 1936. The train is composed entirely of LTSR non-corridor stock. The last LTSR engine of this class, *Thundersley*, was withdrawn in 1952 and the last LMS example in 1960.

[*E. R. Wethersett*

LOWER LEFT: A scene at Plaistow shed on April 6, 1935. Nearest the camera is one of the two LTSR 0-6-0s, the only tender engines the company owned. Class 2F No 22899 was built in 1899 and was intended for the Ottoman Railway in Turkey but was not delivered. It was withdrawn in 1936 having outlived its sister by three years. Next in the row is standard Fowler LMS class 3F 0-6-0T No 16580, MR Johnson class 1P 0-4-4T No 1290 and three LMS built Whitelegg class 3P 4-4-2Ts Nos 2119, 2125 and 2129.

[*E. R. Wethersett*

North Staffordshire

J. H. Adams "K" class 4-4-2T No. 13, later LMS No 2184, waits to leave Derby with a train for Stoke-on-Trent in 1924. It is perhaps appropriate that No 13 is chosen to start this section as it was the fleet of 192 NSR engines that were first to become extinct of all the larger companies engines in the LMS. There were seven "K" class engines built at Stoke-on-Trent works in 1911-12.

[*T. G. Hepburn*

UPPER LEFT: J. H. Adams "K" class 3P 4-4-2T No 2181 accelerates out of Derby with a train for Stoke-on-Trent in 1925. The last of these seven engines was withdrawn in 1935.
[T. G. Hepburn

LOWER LEFT: Hookham "F" class 4P 0-6-4T No 2053 stands in Derby station on a gloomy day in 1930. There were eight of these large tank engines built between 1916 and 1919 and withdrawal came between 1934 and 1936.
[T. G. Hepburn

UPPER RIGHT: One of the six Adams "L" class 3F 0-6-2Ts, No 2246 passes through Longport as it nears Stoke-on-Trent with an up goods in the early 1930s. Introduced in 1903 there were eventually 30 engines in this class, the other 24 being known as the "New L" class which were built between 1908 and 1923. The last loco was withdrawn when four were sold to Lancashire Associated Collieries in 1937. LMS No 2271 sold in this batch has since been preserved as NSR No 2 after having worked at Walkden under the name *Princess* for many years.
[F. R. Hebron

RIGHT: One of the "New L" class 3F 0-6-2Ts sold to Lancashire Associated Collieries, *Sir Robert,* is seen shunting at Mossley Common Colliery on January 18, 1962. This was former LMS No 2262 and was built at Stoke-on-Trent works in 1920.

[*J. R. Carter*

UPPER LEFT: J. H. Adams "G" class 4-4-0 No 86, later LMS No 595, halts at Llandudno Junction with a summer Saturday Stoke-on-Trent-Llandudno express in 1924. There were four of these handsome 4-4-0s built in 1910 at Stoke-on-Trent works. There was only one other 4-4-0 owned by the NSR and this was "KT" class engine No 38 which was originally intended to be a "K" class Atlantic tank. It was built in 1912 and survived to 1933 outliving the other 4-4-0s. *[F. R. Hebron*

LOWER LEFT: Adams "G" class 2P 4-4-0 No 5410, previously LMS No 595, is seen again in May 1928 after having been renumbered to make way for some new Fowler class 2P 4-4-0s then under construction. It is calling at Rudyard with a Macclesfield-Uttoxeter Churnet Valley local formed of LNWR stock shortly before it was withdrawn. *[F. R. Hebron*

North London

The well-known NLR 0-4-2 crane saddle tank is seen at Devons Road shed, Bow in 1926. This engine was originally built as an 0-4-0ST by Sharp Stewart in 1858 for the North & South Western Junction Railway and it was rebuilt as a crane tank in 1872. It survived in this form until scrapped in 1951 and was one of 109 NLR engines to come into LMS ownership. Bearing the No 2896 in the LNWR list it was soon to be given the LMS No 7217. The LNWR took over responsibility for working North London services in 1909 but only a handful of NLR engines were given North Western numbers at that time, the majority were absorbed into the LNWR stock list in 1923 and carried these numbers until the LMS finally got round to renumbering the few that remained in traffic. *[F. R. Hebron*

ABOVE: William Adams NLR 4-4-0T No 2874, allocated LMS No 6435, pulls always from signals at Greenwood box in 1924 with empty stock of a Broad Street-New Barnet train being worked forward to Potters Bar. The four-wheel coaches which form this train were built by the LNWR at Wolverton in 1910 for the Broad Street-Richmond line. Four of these inside cylinder 4-4-0Ts of 1865-69 survived at the grouping and No 2874, formerly NLR No 109, was the last to be withdrawn in 1925.
[F. R. Hebron

UPPER RIGHT: Park NLR 4-4-0T No 2828, later LMS class 1P No 6458, leaves Palmers Green with the 10.45 am Broad Street-Gordon Hill train in 1925 formed of rather more elderly NLR four-wheelers. This class introduced in 1886 totalled 74 engines all of which came into the LMS. They were quickly scrapped and the last went in 1929.
[F. R. Hebron

LOWER RIGHT: The 5.22 pm Broad Street-Potters Bar fast train passes Wood Green in 1925 hauled by Park NLR 4-4-0T No 2828, allocated LMS No 6490. This train which ran fast to New Barnet often caused embarrassment to the LNER's 5.30 pm Kings Cross-Newcastle express.
[F. R. Hebron

Glasgow & South Western

Peter Drummond "51" class 4F 2-6-0 No 17829 heads a Carlisle-Glasgow via Dumfries class H goods train near Rockcliffe just south of the border in the summer of 1936. No 17829, one of eleven built in 1915, was the last surviving Glasgow & South Western Railway tender engine when withdrawn in 1947. The 527 engines to come into LMS ownership from this railway were withdrawn fairly quickly and only one other class of Drummond 0-6-2Ts survived after 1937.

[*E. E. Smith*

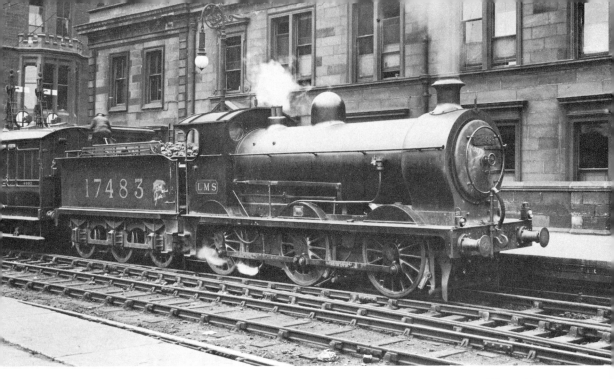

Manson "115" class 3F 0-6-0 No 17483 is pictured in the pre-1928 freight engine livery whilst waiting to leave Glasgow St Enoch with an express in 1926. It was one of 23 fitted with larger boilers out of the class of 36 built in 1900-1910. *[T. G. Hepburn*

Manson "238" class 1F rebuild of James Stirling "635" class 0-4-2 No 17047 awaits its fate inside Perth shed in 1926. Originally introduced in 1874 thirty were rebuilt by Manson in 1901-3. *[T. G. Hepburn*

LEFT: Manson class 1P 6ft 9½in 4-4-0 No 14195 runs light near Ayr against a backcloth of smoking chimneys in the mid 1920s. A total of 57 engines of this class were built between 1892 and 1904.
[*J. Clarke, courtesy M. W. Earley*

BELOW: Manson class 1P 6ft 1¼in 4-4-0 No 14206 leaves Dumfries with a north-bound express from Carlisle in the mid 1920s. There were 25 of these engines built between 1895 and 1899, six were later rebuilt with larger boilers. The last example of the class was withdrawn in 1932. [*J. Clarke, courtesy M. W. Earley*

RIGHT: Smellie class 1P 6ft 1¼in 4-4-0 No 14116 stands outside Corkerhill shed on August 29, 1929. Built in 1882 it was the first of a class of 22 engines, 13 of which were later rebuilt with larger domed boilers (see page after next).

[C. D. E. Roper Nunn, courtesy LCGB

BELOW: One of the larger Manson "337" class 2P 6ft 9½in 4-4-0s, No 14376 in post 1927 black livery, heads a Glasgow-Ayr stopping train near Prestwick in the late 1920s. Thirteen of these engines were built in 1907-1912 and the last survivor was scrapped in 1932. Note the modern appearance of the tender attached to this engine.

[J. Clarke, courtesy M. W. Earley

Manson G & SWR "495" class 4-6-0 No 503, later LMS class 3P No 14664, waits to leave Glasgow St Enoch with an express for Carlisle via Dumfries in 1926. There were two varieties of Manson 4-6-0, 17 of this type built in 1903-11 and two of the "512" class built in 1911. All had gone by the end of 1934. [*T. G. Hepburn*

Manson class 1P 6ft 9½in 4-4-0 No 14199 backs out of Glasgow St Enoch after arrival with a stopping train in 1926. The last of these 57 engines were withdrawn in 1933. [*T. G. Hepburn*

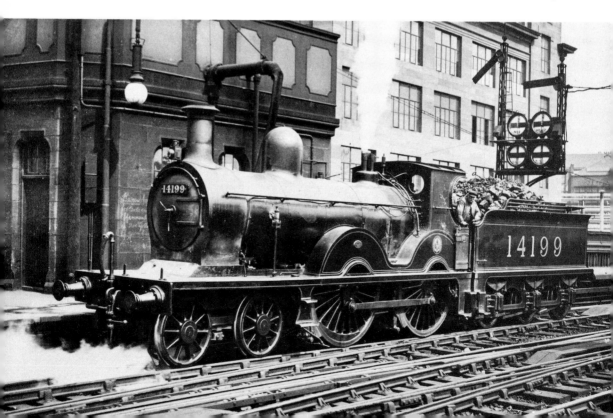

Still resplendent in G & SWR livery, R. H. Whitelegg "540" class 4-6-4T No 544, later LMS class 5P No 15404, waits to leave Glasgow St Enoch in 1926 with an express for Ayr. Six of these impressive machines were built in 1922 but no doubt due to being such a numerically small class they were all withdrawn in 1934-5.

[T. G. Hepburn

One of the 13 Smellie 6ft 1¼in 4-4-0s rebuilt with a larger domed boiler, class 2P No 14118 stands in a centre road at Glasgow St Enoch in 1926. The class became extinct in 1934.

[T. G. Hepburn

Highland

ABOVE: Jones "Skye Bogie" class 1P 4-4-0 No 14284 enters Kyle of Lochalsh with the 10.20 am mail train from Inverness on May 21, 1926. Nine of these engines were built at Lochgorm works for service on the Kyle line between 1882 and 1901. No 14284 was one of four built after David Jones had retired and was fitted with a plain Drummond chimney.
[*C. D. E. Roper Nunn, courtesy LCGB*

LEFT: The pioneer "Skye Bogie", No 14277, shunts on the quayside at Kyle of Lochalsh on April 12, 1926.
[*C. D. E. Roper Nunn, courtesy LCGB*

RIGHT: Jones "Loch" class 2P 4-4-0 No 14384 *Loch Laggan* pilots a Drummond "Castle" class 4-6-0 out of Blair Atholl for the arduous sixteen mile climb to Druimauchdar summit with a Glasgow-Inverness train about 1930. Loch Laggan, which has lost its smokebox wingplates, was one of fifteen "Loch" class engines built by Dubs and Co. in 1896.

[*T. G. Hepburn*

BELOW: Resplendent in Highland livery ,"Loch" class 4-4-0 No 70 *Loch Ashie,* later LMS No 14394, stands in Tain station in September 1923. It was one of three further engines built to this design by the North British Locomotive Company in 1917, no less than 21 years after the previous fifteen !

[*C. D. E. Roper Nunn, courtesy LCGB*

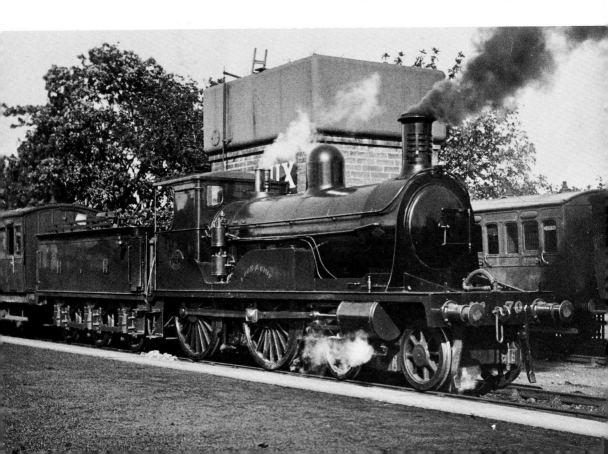

In early LMS days ten Jones "Loch" class 4-4-0s were rebuilt with larger boilers of Caledonian origin. No 14392 *Loch Naver* is seen in this condition leaving Hermitage Tunnel near Dunkeld with a Perth-Blair Atholl local in the early 1930s. Two of these rebuilds survived to come into British Railways ownership, the last to be withdrawn was *Loch Tay* in 1950.

[*F. R. Hebron*

Another Highland design to receive Caledonian boilers were the later survivors of Peter Drummond's "Small Ben" class 2P 4-4-0. No 14409 *Ben Alisky* works out its last months on station pilot duties at Helmsdale in 1949. The last of the twenty "Small Ben" 4-4-0s, *Ben Alder* was withdrawn in 1953 and was stored awaiting preservation until it was quietly dispatched to the breakers in the late 1960s.   [*A. B. MacLeod*

The last surviving Drummond "Large Ben" class 2P 4-4-0 No 14422 *Ben a'Chaoruinn* stands in Elgin station with a Keith-Forres train in 1936, a year before it was withdrawn. There were only six engines of this design and they were all built in 1908/9, ten years after the first of the "Small Ben" class.   [*F. R. Hebron*

UPPER LEFT: Undoubtedly the most famous of all Highland engines were the fifteen 4-6-0 goods engines designed by David Jones and built by Sharp Stewart in 1894. No 115, later LMS No 17928, sits outside Aviemore shed on August 27, 1923.

[C. D. E. Roper Nunn, courtesy LCGB

LOWER LEFT: "Jones Goods" class 4F 4-6-0 No 17929, fitted with a plain chimney in place of the distinctive louvred design, is seen on the turntable inside the Inverness roundhouse in the spring of 1936 complete with a small wooden HR snow-plough.

[E. E. Smith

ABOVE: The first 4-6-0 to run in the British Isles, "Jones Goods" No 103 marshals a southbound pick-up goods at Ballinluig in Highland days. Withdrawn in 1934 as LMS No 17916 it was preserved in HR livery. In 1959 it was brought out of store at St Rollox and returned to working order to haul some special trains to the Scottish Industries Exhibition that year. No 103 was kept in traffic for working special trains until 1965 when it was placed in the Glasgow Museum of Transport. Note that even at the early date of this picture No 103 had already lost its smokebox wingplates.   [*Locomotive Publishing Co.*

LEFT: Peter Drummond "Castle" class 3P 4-6-0 No 14684 *Duncraig Castle* climbs steadily up the 1 in 60 gradient towards Slochd summit with an Inverness-Perth stopping train in 1937. No 14684 was from the first series of twelve "Castles" built between 1900 and 1911 by Dubs and NBL. A further four with detail differences were turned out by NBL in 1913.

[*F. R. Hebron*

BELOW: A final three "Castles" were built by NBL in 1917, these had the driving wheel diameter increased by three inches to six feet and were fitted with six-wheel tenders. No 14691 *Brodie Castle* makes a smoky departure from Perth with an Inverness train in the mid 1920s. The train is a typical Highland mixture of the period with Midland, Highland, LNW and standard LMS carriages.

[*Locomotive Publishing Co.*

UPPER LEFT: An unidentified Cumming "Clan goods" class 5F 4-6-0 pilots a Drummond "Small Ben" 4-4-0 out of Kyle of Lochalsh with an Inverness train in 1937. There were eight of these mixed traffic engines which were introduced in 1918, thus preceding by one year the "Clan" 4-6-0s from which they derived their name. For many years they were the largest engines permitted on the Kyle line and six came into BR ownership, the last surviving until 1952. The HR shunting signal in this view controls the exit from the engine shed and turntable road. [F. R. Hebron

LOWER LEFT: Christopher Cumming's first design for the Highland Railway was the very neat "Snaigow" class of 4-4-0 for the Inverness-Wick route in 1916. No 73 Snaigow, later LMS class 3P No 14522, leaves Wick shed before working the 2.30 pm train for Inverness on March 1, 1924. Only two of these engines were built and both were withdrawn by the end of 1936. [C. D. E. Roper Nunn, courtesy LCGB

BELOW: Cumming "Clan" class 4P 4-6-0 No 14763 Clan Fraser impatiently awaits departure from Callander with an evening Glasgow-Oban express in the mid 1930s. Allocated to St Rollox depot it was one of several "Clans" exiled from the Highland main line by the introduction of the Stanier "Black Fives". Eight examples of this class were built, all by Hawthorn Leslie as were all the other Cumming engines. [T. G. Hepburn

BELOW: P. Drummond class 0P 0-4-4T No 15051, formerly named *Strathpeffer*, waits at The Mound with the morning Dornoch branch train in 1949. Four of these diminutive tanks were built at Lochgorm in 1905-6 and the first withdrawal took place in 1930. However, No 15053 survived until 1956 and became the last of 150 Highland engines which were allocated LMS numbers after the grouping.
[A. B. MacLeod

Caledonian

McIntosh "49" class 4P 4-6-0 No 14750 leaves Perth with the 5.30 pm Aberdeen-Glasgow, the one time "Grampian Express", in July 1926. As can be seen from the Caledonian route indicator the train is routed via Coatbridge into Glasgow Central in order to provide good connections with the night trains to the south. There were only two engines built to this design, forerunners of the "Cardean" class and when built at Saint Rollox in 1903 they were the most powerful express engines in the country. Withdrawal of both took place in 1933. The first coach is one of the well-known CR "Grampian" twelve-wheelers first introduced in 1905 and is a brake third whilst the second coach is a CR eight-wheel composite. The third is a Pullman dining car, one of an eventual total of sixteen Pullman cars which ran on CR routes from 1914 onwards. All were sold to the LMS in 1933 and the author observed one still in use in 1959 on an Inverness-Kyle of Lochalsh train.   [*Locomotive Publishing Co.*

ABOVE: Most famous of all the 1,107 (including 30 built by the LMS) engines of Caledonian design to come into the LMS were J. F. McIntosh's series of "Dunalastair" 4-4-0s. "Dunalastair II" class 2P 4-4-0 No 14335, formerly named *Breadalbane*, waits to leave Motherwell with a stopping train for Glasgow Central on August 2, 1938. The fifteen engines of this class were all built in 1897. [L. Hanson

LEFT: McIntosh "Dunalastair IV" class 2P 4-4-0 No 14351 passes the ticket platform as it storms out of Perth with an Aberdeen-Glasgow Buchanan Street train about 1930. Nineteen of these engines were built between 1904 and 1910 and they were the final development of the saturated "Dunalastair" 4-4-0s first introduced in 1896. Two were later rebuilt by Pickersgill (see next page). [T. G. Hepburn

UPPER LEFT: A pair of McIntosh "Dunalastair III" class 2P 4-4-0s, with No 14348 leading, prepare to leave Callander with a special train for Dunblane in 1936. *[E. E. Smith*

LOWER LEFT: "Dunalastair IV" superheated rebuild, class 3P 4-4-0 No 14439, allocated to Carstairs shed, heads a southbound coal train near Uddingston on August 23, 1947. No 14439 survived to be the last of all the 87 McIntosh 4-4-0s when withdrawn from the Highland section in 1958. *[E. R. Wethersett*

ABOVE: McIntosh "139" class 3P 4-4-0 No 14452 accelerates away from Perth with a Dundee-Glasgow train in the mid 1920s. The leading three coaches are all still in the Caledonian purple-lake and white livery. These 4-4-0s, sometimes known as the "Dunalastair IV Superheater" class, were built between 1910 and 1914, only 21 came into LMS ownership as one had been destroyed in the Quintinshill disaster of 1915. *[Locomotive Publishing Co.*

ABOVE: Pickersgill "72" class 3P 4-4-0 No 14490, in crimson lake livery, departs from Aberdeen with a local train for Perth in July 1926. The four passenger coaches are of Lambie CR origin whilst the last vehicle is an LNWR full brake.

[Locomotive Publishing Co

RIGHT: Sister Pickersgill 4-4-0 No 14491 struggles to get a southbound un-fitted goods moving out of Perth during the immediate post World War II locomotive shortage, August 2, 1945.

[Neville Fields

BELOW: No 14487 approaches Moncrieff tunnel as it leaves Perth with a Dundee-Glasgow express in 1930. Pickersgill built a total of 48 4-4-0s between 1916 and 1922, all basically similar and the last example survived until 1963.

[T. G. Hepburn

UPPER RIGHT: J. F. McIntosh produced six designs of 4-6-0 for the Caledonian which in total numbered 42 engines. None of them were anything like as successful as his "Dunalastair" series of 4-4-0s. The first class to appear were the "55" class built for use on the difficult Callander and Oban line. McIntosh "Oban Bogie" class 4P 4-6-0 No 14603 passes under a fine Calendonian signal gantry as it leaves Stirling with a Glasgow Buchanan Street train in 1926. They only outlived the original Brittain "Oban Bogies" by seven years, the last of the nine being withdrawn in 1937.   [T. G. Hepburn

LOWER RIGHT: In 1916 William Pickersgill introduced his "60" class 4-6-0 of which six were built. After the grouping the LMS had a further twenty of these engines built with slightly larger cylinders. Class 3P 4-6-0 No 14633, of the LMS built series, enters Stirling with a northbound troop train formed entirely of LNWR stock on July 14, 1938. [J. P. Wilson

BELOW: The best 4-6-0s the Caledonian had were almost certainly the six "River" class 4-6-0s designed by F. G. Smith for the Highland Railway. They were found to be too heavy for that railway and they were sold to the Caledonian after only two had been delivered to the HR by Hawthorn Leslie in 1915. No 14759, now LMS class 4P, enters Perth General with a train from Glasgow about 1930. The leading coach is an LNWR double-ended brake, a one time slip coach, whilst the second vehicle is of LYR origin.   [T. G. Hepburn

McIntosh "139" class 3P 4-4-0 No 14447 and a Pickersgill class 3P 4-4-0 make a fine sight as they depart from Aberdeen joint station with a Glasgow express in the mid 1920s. The smokebox wingplates gave these engines a truly massive appearance but they were soon removed by the LMS

[*Locomotive Publishing Co.*

LEFT: Dugald Drummond class 1P 4-4-0 No 14114, in crimson lake livery, poses in 1926 beside the gasometer that appears in so many photographs taken at Stirling. It was one of a class of twelve engines originally built for the Clyde Coast route. Eight came into LMS ownership and all were gone by the end of 1930.
[*T. G. Hepburn*

BELOW: McIntosh "812" class 3F 0-6-0 No 17572 heads out of Perth with a southbound mixed freight about 1930. The first three vans are of LNWR origin whilst the other three are LYR, standard LMS and Midland respectively. The "812" class 0-6-0s were introduced in 1899 and a total of 96 were built in ten years and all but three survived to British Railways ownership. [*T. G. Hepburn*

ABOVE: Pickersgill "191" class 3P 4-6-0 No 14620 cautiously descends Glencruitten bank with the 9.45 am Glasgow Buchanan Street-Oban express in June 1925. At the rear of the train can be seen the Pullman observation car "Maid of Morven" introduced on this route in 1914 and was the only Pullman of its type until the "Devon Belle" cars entered service after World War II. It was sold in company with the other 15 Caledonian Pullmans to the LMS in 1933 and was scrapped by 1938.   [*C. D. E. Roper Nunn, courtesy LCGB*

RIGHT: Brittain "Oban Bogie" class 1P 4-4-0 No 14104 pilots Pickersgill "191" class 3P 4-6-0 No 14620 out of Oban up the 1 in 50 gradient of Glencruitten bank with the 5 pm Glasgow express on April 23, 1925. There were ten engines built to George Brittain's "Oban Bogie" design and all were built in 1882. The eight Pickersgill 4-6-0s of class "191" were built in 1922 for the Oban line but proved to be rather under-boilered.

[*C. D. E. Roper Nunn, courtesy LCGB*

ABOVE: Eugene Drummond 'Jumbo' class 2F 0-6-0 No 17562 passes through Gretna with a northbound loose-coupled goods in the early 1930s. The Drummond "Jumbos" were numerically the largest class on the Caledonian with 244 examples built between 1883 and 1897. All came into LMS ownership and 238 survived nationalisation in 1948.
[F. R. Hebron

tender first with an Officers special from Glasgow in June 1925. The leading coach is Caledonian family day saloon No 1, whilst the second coach is an LNWR six-berth family saloon of a type designed by C. A. Park at Wolverton in 1898. Both vehicles are still in their pre-grouping livery.
[C. D. E. Roper Nunn, courtesy LCGB

ABOVE: One of the twelve Pickersgill "944" class 4P 4-6-2Ts built in 1917, No 15352, passes Ibrox with a down stopping train on July 12, 1938. This class ended its days on banking duties at Beattock, the last engine being withdrawn in 1953.　　[J. P. Wilson

CENTRE LEFT: McIntosh "439" class 2P 0-4-4T No 15168 is seen at Crieff with a Comrie-Perth train formed of an LNWR push pull set in spring 1937. [E. E. Smith

LOWER LEFT: Lambie class 1P 4-4-0T No 15025 runs light at Connel Ferry in spring 1937 when it was the Ballachulish branch engine. Twelve of these tanks were built in 1893 for working the Glasgow Central underground line and the class became extinct in 1938.
　　[E. E. Smith

Class 2P 0-4-4T No 15233 nears Killin Junction with the one coach Killin branch train from Loch Tay in spring 1937. This was the final version of the McIntosh 0-4-4T first introduced in 1895 and was from a batch of 14 built under Pickersgill's direction between 1915 and 1922. Ten further engines were built by the LMS in 1925 bringing the total to 136.   [E. E. Smith

The last surviving Dugald Drummond class 1P 0-4-4T No 15103 approaches Wick with the 2.40 pm mixed train from Lybster on August 22, 1935. One of 24 built between 1884 and 1891 it survived until the Lybster branch was closed in 1944.   [K. A. C. R. Nunn, courtesy LCGB

End of the line. The Killin branch engine, Caledonian class 2P 0-4-4T No 15233, stands outside the single road Loch Tay engine shed on a spring morning in 1937.   *[E. E. Smith*